BBC MUSIC GUIDES

HAYDN STRING QUARTETS

BBC MUSIC GUIDES

BBC MUSIC GUIDES

HAYDN
STRING QUARTETS

ROSEMARY HUGHES

BRITISH BROADCASTING CORPORATION

Published by the British Broadcasting Corporation
35 Marylebone High Street, London WIM 4AA

ISBN: 0 563 06808 6

First published 1966

Reprinted 1969, 1972, 1975, 1976, 1980

Printed in England by The Garden City Press Limited
Letchworth, Hertfordshire SG6 1JS

THE ORIGINS: STRINGS IN FOUR PARTS
HAYDN'S OP. 1 & 2

Haydn's string quartets are, of all his works, the most faithful mirror of his human and artistic personality and the most complete chronicle of his growth as a composer, since they span the entire half-century of his creative life. But they are more than that. 'Haydn and the string quartet were young together', said Marion Scott, that great pioneer of Haydn research, in the hundredth number of 'Music Magazine'; and it was in his hands, and as part of the process of achieving his full maturity and stature as a composer, that the string quartet, as we know it, finally came into being.

'The string quartet as we know it': four stringed instruments – two violins, viola, cello – equal and independent, yet so intimately interacting that their texture constitutes a unique medium, endless in its expressive possibilities and in its resources of sheer sound. But in the 1750s, when the young Haydn first began to earn his living as a musician, this had barely begun to be reckoned with among all the possible groupings in the world of instrumental music. It was not, of course, that composition for strings in four parts was unknown; on the contrary, it had long been recognized, in theory and practice, as the basic texture of all concerted instrumental writing. It was represented by two generations of Italian composers, from Alessandro Scarlatti to Tartini, Sammartini and Galuppi, in a long line of works labelled *sinfonia a quattro* or *concerto a quattro*. It was current coin among the progressive group of composers centred on the court of the Elector Palatine at Mannheim and headed by Johann Stamitz, as also among Bavarian and Austrian composers, especially in the cheerful, popular suites of dance tunes which were being composed for informal enjoyment. But all this music was conceived in the first instance, not in terms of four solo instruments, but of orchestral strings, with their conductor at the harpsichord, directing and indeed completing the performance by his amplification of the harmonies implied by the shorthand system of figures below the bass line. *Basso continuo* it was called, and in these works the bass line moves with a firm, unbroken tread, while the violin melodies are of orchestral cut, and the viola, where not in octaves with the bass, has a purely subordinate part. As for the cello, it has no voice, as such, at all, for its identity is merged with the double bass which, in every orchestra, then as now, was the foundation of the bass line. It is true that in fugal movements all four parts achieve equal importance; but fugal technique and texture were already outmoded and were being rapidly supplanted by the more elegant and expressive melodiousness of the so-called *galant* style.

There were exceptions. In northern Germany the polyphonic 'quartet sonata', on the lines of the baroque trio sonata – that is, for two violins, viola and 'basso' (cello or gamba with harpsichord continuo) – was regarded by Quantz, Telemann and their contemporaries as 'the touchstone of the genuine contrapuntist'; but this, although genuine chamber music, was irrevocably tied to the harpsichord continuo, so that the cello could never achieve its freedom. Far more important was the work of certain members of the Mannheim group, especially Johann Stamitz and his son Karl, and Franz Xaver Richter, in whose *quatuors*, alongside those orchestrally conceived, we find elaborate and lyrical writing for all four strings – the bass specifically a cello – which is clearly conceived in terms of solo instruments and which, by the very manner of writing for the cello, shakes itself loose from the continuo. Certain Italians, notably Galuppi, were working along similar lines, and in the next decade Boccherini went even further in this direction. Here the string quartet is almost in being; all that was needed to consolidate it and make it viable was a closer and more continuous integration of the individual parts. But their very richness was a structural weakness. In these *concertante* quartets (*concertino a quattro* was another name for them) the four parts behave indeed as if for four concerto soloists, and lack the concentration needed for unified development, whether of texture or of the actual musical material.

But to Haydn at eighteen (he was born in 1732), newly dismissed from St Stephen's Cathedral choir and thrown on his own resources in the Vienna of the 1750s, all this rich and varied world of music-making was unknown or out of reach; the immediate problem was how to make ends meet, and for that purpose there were serious gaps in his equipment. Neither his village home and early schooling nor his ten years as a chorister at St Stephen's had given him more than a smattering of all-round education, nor had he received more than a nominal lesson or two in musical theory. All he had been systematically taught was to sing and to play the violin. For the rest, his musical equipment consisted of such counterpoint as he had managed to teach himself on his own account with the aid of a textbook, and the musical experience and repertory that any choirboy absorbs in the course of ten years' continuous performance of liturgical music. Besides this, for the boys of St Stephen's choir, there was a certain amount of operatic and other festive secular music, since they were frequently sent for to perform on cere-monial occasions at the Imperial Court.

It is worth considering for a moment what music would thus have come to be the furniture of the young Haydn's mind. Not Bach or Handel, though these were at the height of their powers, for neither distant England nor provincial, Lutheran Leipzig would have had any musical traffic with the Imperial capital. But the great Italian musical idiom which formed Handel's style was the international language of music: that of the Italian composers who came and went within the Habsburg Empire, and of their Austrian contemporaries, whether working for the church, the opera house or the ceremonies of the Court. And in the Cathedral (especially during Lent when orchestral instruments were forbidden) he encountered the sixteenth-century polyphonic style of Palestrina, long abandoned in common musical speech but preserved as an ancient and vener-able ecclesiastical tongue; here, moreover, it was still used as a living language by the great Johann Joseph Fux, Court *Kapellmeister*, whose noble Masses were sung at St Stephen's and with whose classic textbook, the *Gradus ad Parnassum*, he had already wrestled unaided as a choirboy.

But, with this world now closed to him, the only way to make a living was by teaching or casual performing jobs. And for eight years he did in fact spend his days 'trailing wretchedly around giving lessons to children' (his own expression) and half his nights still trying to teach himself to compose. There remained the evenings; and here there was music-making in plenty, unofficial but lively, where a competent violinist could on occasion earn himself the price of a meal. An eighteenth-century Viennese almanac (quoted by Karl Geiringer in his life of Haydn)[1] gives some account of it:

> On fine summer nights you may come upon serenades in the streets at all hours. They are not, as in Italy, a mere matter of a singer and a guitar. Here serenades are not meant for declarations of love, for which the Viennese have better opportunities. Such night music may be given by a trio or a quartet of wind instruments, and works of some extent may be played ... however late a serenade is given, all windows are soon filled and in a few minutes the musicians are surrounded by an applauding crowd.

As an old man, Haydn would recall playing in such serenading parties; from playing in them to composing for them would have been a natural step. He himself told his biographer August Griesinger, fifty years later, that the first impetus towards writing for quartet of strings was given by a summer invitation from a certain Baron von Fürnberg, in whose house he had been giving music lessons, since the little group that met in the evenings for music-making at the Baron's country house on the Danube consisted of four players – the Baron's steward, the parish priest, a local cellist and himself. But whether it was for this domestic party or for some team of his own in Vienna that he wrote his first *Divertimenti a quattro*, as he himself called them, his use of this term reveals their kinship with the four-part divertimenti of his older contemporaries in Bavaria and Austria: men with unfamiliar names like Zach and Camerloher and Starzer, whose music was tuneful and popular and who were therefore looked down on by the austerer North Germans for preferring dance-tunes to counterpoint.

Twelve of Haydn's little *divertimenti a quattro* survive from this epoch.[2] Various publishers subsequently packaged them into opus numbers, six to a set, as 'Op. 1' and 'Op. 2', and this is still the most convenient label for them (eighteenth-century opus numbers were labels attached by publishers, not composers). What distinguishes them already from the dance suites and

[1] *Haydn: A Creative Life in Music*, second edition (Allen & Unwin, 1964), p. 29.

[2] Thirteen, if we include the little E flat Divertimento discovered independently by Marion Scott and Karl Geiringer as having been the original 'Op. 1, no. 1' in some early editions; but the present Op. 1, no 5, is really a displaced symphony, so that the two cancel each other out.

divitimenti which Haydn already knew is their balanced five-movement symmetry. His inborn sense of design, instead of stringing his little movements together at random, has grouped them around the slow movement as centrepiece, ornate and lyrical, with a dance tune, in the form of a minuet, on either side of it, and a lively *allegro* or *presto* at the beginning and end. This is the pattern of all but three of the quartets of his Op. 1 and Op. 2. What further distinguishes them is that, although they are conceived in terms of a little orchestra, it is an orchestra which is ready to break up into its component parts, setting upper strings against lower, outer against middle, or throwing some little motive or accompanying figure from one instrument to another. What Haydn is evolving in his imagination and practice is a special divertimento texture, open and translucent, distinct from the normal orchestral texture of the period as we see it in his contemporaries' work or in his own earliest symphonies. (These were composed only a few years later, for in 1759 he got his first full-time job in charge of an orchestra, as *Kapellmeister* to a Bohemian nobleman, Count Morzin.) It is a texture in which, although the double-bass is still the foundation of the bass line, the continuity of the bass line itself is repeatedly broken by the airy cross-talk between the instruments, and *basso continuo* and harpsichord are gradually edged out of the picture.

Before we start to look more closely at the music itself, a couple of paragraphs on its technical foundations (which can be skipped by experienced listeners) may be found helpful by the untrained music-lover, and for two reasons. A technical term is often the simplest way of describing a thing: thus, to speak of the key in which a piece is written as the 'tonic' is to use one word where otherwise one would be forced to use half a dozen. Moreover, where the inner life of a musical work – its design, its detailed structure, its emotional impact on the listener – springs from certain fundamental facts or laws, a recognition of those laws brings us nearer to the heart of the music; whereas, if they are ignored, we are left with nothing but vague feelings and rhapsodizings.

Briefly then: the music of Europe from the immediate predecessors of Bach and Handel to the immediate successors of Brahms is based on keys, major and minor, and their relationship to each other. Any piece of that epoch, whether large or small, major or minor, has a home key (with its key-note) or 'tonic', and is said to be 'in' that key – D major, C minor and the rest. But it need not and will not stay in that key for its entire course. It will move out towards other keys: readily and easily to those based on the notes of its own scale, and most readily, and with the strongest 'pull' to the key based on the fifth of its own scale, known as the 'dominant'.

Another close link is that of a major scale with the minor scale starting on the same note as key-note, or 'tonic minor'; but this is a deeper change, since it alters the character and harmonies of the tonic itself. (Lovers of Schubert will not need to be reminded what heart-rending use he repeatedly makes of this relationship.) A transformation of another kind happens where the composer, taking his key-note, no longer as tonic, but as, say, the third of a new key, uses it as a pivot on which to swing round into this key. The resulting key change (or 'modulation') will be felt as a move into remote, alien territory, and will give the listener a corresponding sense of strangeness, even of drama or mystery. There are many other key relationships and many other possible modulations, close or remote; the whole system of classical tonality (and a number of the changes and trends succeeding it in the present century) is admirably described for music-lovers in Robert L. Jacobs's *Harmony for the Listener*.[1] All that it is possible to suggest here is that its resources can be used by the composer for purposes of design: to achieve movement (e.g. from tonic to dominant and back) or contrast (first section in the major, middle section in the tonic minor, return of first section in the major). They can also be used to produce various forms of emotional impact: pathos, mystery, the building up and release of tension. (A familiar and superb instance of the last-named is the bridge passage, in Beethoven's Fifth Symphony, between the C minor of the scherzo and the C major of the last movement.)

Now the instrumental music with which the young Haydn was acquainted uses these key relationships on broad, simple lines; and so, accordingly, does his own. The first movements of his

[1] Oxford University Press, 1958. A brilliant and succinct summary is also given by Sir Donald Tovey in the Introduction to. Vol I of his *Essays in Musical Analysis* (O.U.P., 1935).

little divertimento-quartets are nearly all in lively tempo, and follow the course that was gaining currency as the normal first-movement pattern: two sections, each repeated, of unequal length, the first opening in the tonic, and moving out to a fresh key centre (in a major key, almost invariably the dominant), usually on a fresh group of themes; and the second and longer section moving back again, through various expansions and modulations based on the earlier material, to the home tonic, in which the opening section (or part of it) is recapitulated, with such modifications of detail as are needed to keep it in the tonic key throughout. Such, baldly stated, is the outline of that 'first-movement form' (or 'sonata form') which underlies first movements as disparate in size and power as those of these tiny quartets and Beethoven's first Razumovsky or the great works of Haydn's later years. What was needed, to bring tension and momentum to this bare outline, was a grasp of the dramatic possibilities inherent in key relationships, so that the move away from, or back to, the home key could become an event, not a mere piece of pattern-making; and also, a capacity in the themes themselves to grow, evolve and change: in other words, to develop. Haydn's earliest works are for the most part still in the pattern-making stage. The themes are repeated in sequential scroll-work, not expanded or transformed, and the return to the home key is uneventful because it has never receded below the horizon – like a short country walk always within sight of one's own house. But there are signs, here and there, that he is beginning to sense the possibilities of organic growth and of drama behind the pattern. In the first movement of Op. 2, no. 1, in A major, the opening theme is little more than a formula; but it contains a rhythmic figure (*x*) which, with its forward impulse, was to become a fingerprint of his (in the London symphonies, the last quartets, *The Creation*):

On this he bases his middle or development section, and eventually builds with it a bridge of answering phrases to span the gap – admittedly not a very great one – between the key of F sharp minor into which he has steered the music and the approach-road to the return of the tonic, A major, and the opening theme.

Ex. 2   Allegro

And in the F major Quartet, no. 4 of the same set, a succession of abrupt modulations in the development section makes the ear lose its sense of direction, until a reiterated C reveals itself as a familiar landmark and works up an agreeable sense of expectancy until, as a good dominant should, it resolves on to its tonic, F, and we realize that for the past ten bars we have been on the threshold of our own doorstep.

The final movements follow the same pattern as the first, but on an even smaller scale; rapid, lightweight finales were the accepted practice at this period. Where Haydn's finales score, just now, is not in any subtlety of organization, but in a freshness and vitality expressed sometimes through the liveliness and point of the instrumental dialogue, and sometimes in a free and piquant irregularity of phrase length. This asymmetrical turn of phrase was a habit of mind which persisted throughout Haydn's life, and the energy and continuity of his greatest and most highly organized movements owes much to its underlying impetus. It is already apparent in embryo in the sprawling vitality of the opening bars of the last movement of the finale of the D major Quartet Op. 1, no. 3:

Ex. 3

The slow movements, with the exception of the excellent set of variations which opens the B flat Quartet Op. 2, no. 6, are laid out as violin solos in an almost operatic style, with the first violin as prima donna, occasionally in duet with second violin or viola. For the most part their idiom is mellifluous but conventional, and the lower strings have a dull time of it as mere accompanists. But there are touches of poetry and imagination: the muted scoring and pizzicato accompaniment of the charming slow movement of the C major Quartet, Op. 1, no. 6, or the answering phrases between first and second violins in the *adagio* of the G major, no. 4 of the same set. Best of all is the *adagio non troppo* of the F major Quartet, Op. 2, no. 4; it is in the tonic minor, and F minor is to Haydn what G minor is to Mozart, the key of pain and desolation. In the tragic accents of this movement Haydn touches real nobility.

But it is in the minuets of these early quartets that Haydn reveals himself from the very outset in all his originality and vigour and melodic vitality, once again constantly manifested in the freedom and irregularity of his phrase-lengths. The frequent bold, open scoring in octaves between upper and lower strings seems at times to call for a continuo to fill out the harmony (and probably reckoned on one). But there are other movements where it seems purposeful and genuinely imagined: either where the octave passages are contrasted with passages in a different texture, or, more significantly, where Haydn makes use of some contrapuntal device such as canonic imitation. The second minuet of the B flat Quartet, Op. 1, no. 1, shows the use of both these resources.

Ex. 4

This is an effect that would be merely blurred by a continuo. Still less could it find a place in certain of the trio sections, such as the delicious serenading A minor trio of the first minuet of the A major Quartet, Op. 2, no. 1, with its touches of pizzicato. The trios are nearly all in different keys, whether major (usually closely related) or tonic or relative minor, and provide imaginative contrasts of mood and texture.

Within each quartet, the two minuets flanking the central movement are well-differentiated individuals. And in the F major work already mentioned, Op. 2, no., 4, they are unmistakably in different tempi, the leisurely motion and subdivided beat of the first (*a*) in marked contrast with the brisk staccato movement of the second (*b*), to which the cross-rhythms of the trio give an added touch of comedy:

Ex. 5 (a)

These two tempi represent two distinct traditions in regard to the speed and style of the minuet, which have considerable bearing on Haydn's later development. The minuet of the mid-eighteenth century was a dignified dance in moderate tempo, and Haydn wrote a splendid sequence of minuets in this tradition, from these early divertimento quartets to the Paris and London symphonies, as well as in the sets which he wrote as ballroom dances. But there was also an earlier tradition of a different character. A musical dictionary of 1703 writes of the minuet thus: 'One ought, in imitation of the Italians, to use the signature 3–8 or 6–8 to mark its movement, which is always very gay and very fast'. The two minuets of this Quartet provide evidence that Haydn's youthful experience included both minuet traditions. That of the statelier dance allowed of a subdivided beat, giving leisure for semiquaver figures and ornamentation; that of the earlier and faster minuet tradition moves on a crotchet beat, with running quavers as the only subdivision. Throughout Haydn's work these two traditions run side by side, undergoing modification, on the one hand, from the popular and rustic dances – the *Deutsche* and *Ländler* – which he inherited from his Austrian and Bavarian forerunners, and, on the other, from that sublimating process which dance music undergoes when, removed from the dance floor, its essence is distilled in the composer's mind. It is this process which gave us Chopin's waltzes and mazurkas, and which, over the years of Haydn's creative life, was to carry his faster minuet to the boundary of the one-in-a-bar scherzo and beyond.

At this stage, the strongest influence in this process of sublimation was Haydn's powerful and purposeful urge towards counterpoint. This term embraces everything to do with the art and technique of handling music horizontally, as the combination of melodic lines independent in themselves but incidentally producing harmony. The seventeenth and early eighteenth centuries had evolved a technique and a theory of counterpoint, vocal and instrumental, based on the practice of the sixteenth century; we have already seen Haydn at grips with it in his solitary hours with Fux's *Gradus ad Parnassum*. Now we find him putting it to practical use, in tightening the two-part counterpoint of his minuets by a touch of canonic imitation, such as we saw in Ex. 4; another excellent instance is the second minuet of the B flat Quartet, Op. 2, no. 6. Sometimes he goes still further, as in the trio of the second minuet in the G major Quartet, Op. 1, no. 4; it is in G minor, and the canon between the two violins anticipates the famous canonic 'Witches' Minuet' in the D minor Quartet, Op. 76, no. 2, by a good forty years.

Ex. 6

THE STRING QUARTET EMERGES
HAYDN'S OP. 9, 17, AND 20

It is always disconcerting when a familiar landmark is removed, and Haydn-lovers who have known the famous 'Serenade' from Op. 3, no. 5, for as long as they can remember may well feel a sense of loss when they learn that the six quartets known as Haydn's Op. 3 are almost certainly not by Haydn at all, but by a monk named Romanus Hofstetter.[1]

But their elimination from the canon of Haydn's quartets reveals a significant pattern of events – that for close on ten years Haydn wrote no string quartets at all, but that then, in the short space of five years, between 1768 or 1769 and 1772, he composed in quick succession the three sets published as Op. 9, Op. 17 and Op. 20, in which we can watch the string quartet emerging, in substance and in texture, with the swiftness and inevitability of leaves breaking from their buds in a late spring.

Some, at least, of the reasons for the long gap are apparent. After Count Morzin, Haydn's first employer, had disbanded his orchestra, Haydn had almost immediately, in 1761, entered the service of the princely Esterházy family, who maintained a far larger establishment, still further expanded when Prince Nicholas 'the Magnificent' called into existence his vast new palace of Esterháza in 1766. Haydn was thus extended to the limit, not merely composing for the weekly orchestral concerts (he wrote thirty-five symphonies between 1761 and 1770) and other festive occasions, but directing all performances, in palace, chapel or opera-theatre, and rehearsing and coaching singers and instrumentalists. In such a life there was no time and no demand for the little informal divertimenti of his earlier years. But there was a demand for divertimenti of a wholly different kind. Prince Nicholas Esterházy played the baryton, a kind of viola da gamba which, beside the normal bowed gut strings, had metal strings at the back of the neck, which could either be plucked or left to vibrate in acoustic sympathy with the gut strings. It was part of

[1] The evidence is summarized in an article by Alan Tyson and H. C. Robbins Landon, 'Who Composed Haydn's Op. 3 ? ', *Musical Times*, July, 1964.

Haydn's job to compose music for the Prince to play, and in the course of duty he wrote, between 1765 and 1775, no fewer than 126 Trios for baryton, viola and cello – ninety-six of them before 1771. They are for the most part ephemeral little pieces, but their importance in Haydn's development was out of all proportion to their intrinsic value. The task of composing them drove him to think in terms of three individual performers and write for them freely and independently, without harpsichord continuo – for the baryton's plucked strings could fill out the harmonies where necessary – and with the cello providing the bass line. He had already written rich *concertante* parts for solo cello in his early symphonies: in the slow movement of no. 13 and, with the leading violins, in the trilogy *Le Matin*, *Le Midi* and *Le Soir*, nos. 6 to 8, where, as Landon suggests in his great book on Haydn's symphonies, the use of *concertante* strings had given him a freer and more truly 'violinistic' approach to the whole string family.[1] Now he learned to use the cello as bass, while treating it with far more flexibility and freedom than the conventional foundation-bass line permitted, even allowing it, now and then, to sing in its tenor register to a guitar-like accompaniment on the metal strings of the baryton.

But such externals as these are not in themselves enough to account for the creative crisis in which Haydn was caught up between the late sixties and 1772, the year of his fortieth birthday, five years or so in which his art matured with startling speed, both in musical power and originality and in emotional depth. Various reasons for this have been suggested. Many believe that he was affected by the trend towards the expression of subjective emotion in the literature and music of the time, reflected in the 'sensibility' (*Empfindsamkeit*) of Emanuel Bach and the song-writers of these years, and in the tempestuous passions of the early Romantic dramas of the 'Storm and Stress' period. As for his personal life during these years, beyond the fact that his marriage was unhappy, we know little, save that he had a prolonged attack of fever in 1770. But the growth of mind and spirit falls outside the obvious workings of cause and effect; and in those who, like Haydn, develop slowly, it is not uncommon for passion and power and vision to build up beneath a surface of stolid hard work and routine and then, touched off

[1] *The Symphonies of Joseph Haydn* (Rockliff, 1955), p. 238.

by some tiny unexplained impact, break forth all the more powerfully for having been held back.

It is, then, in these few vital years that Haydn's *Divertimenti a quattro* (as he still calls them) become, in all but name, true string quartets. The six of Op. 9 (published in 1771) already differ profoundly from his early divertimento-quartets, in scale, in design and in spirit. They are in four movements, dropping the second minuet of the original divertimento pattern (which, however, leaves its mark in the placing of the minuet as second movement, preceding the *adagio*). The first movements are spacious and deliberate, with a new tempo direction, *moderato*, instead of the earlier *allegro* or *presto*, allowing the beat to subdivide and the figuration characteristic of solo instruments to unfold and breathe. The cello, it is true, is not yet fully emancipated, nor is it certain that Haydn is not still envisaging the presence of a double-bass an octave lower, for at times the viola goes below the cello line even where this is carrying the true bass of the harmony. But, against this, we constantly meet with passages where only a solo cello could match the graceful figuration of the upper instruments. Ex. 7 below, from the first movement of the C major Quartet, Op. 9, no. 1, illustrates this, where (*a*) is the opening theme in C, while (*b*) is the variant of the same theme with which the music swings over and settles down on to the dominant, G major.

Ex. **7** *(a)*

Moderato

This, indeed, is the *concertante* treatment of the strings, comparable to that found in some of the Mannheim composers' work, which had already appeared in Haydn's symphonies. The ustimlus of having a first-rate young violinist, Luigi Tomasini, as friend and orchestra leader, doubtless had something to do with it, and may have been responsible for the brilliance of the first violin parts in many movements of both the Op. 9 and the Op. 17 quartets, with their use of the highest register, their double-stopping and their pauses for cadenzas. Had Haydn taken a wrong turning here, his quartets might have evolved as miniature violin concertos or as panels of decorative tracery, graceful but static.

But the native toughness of his mind and the intuition of genius provided the counterpoise to this tendency, and in two vitally important ways. The first of these was his strong urge to unify his movements by making his initial theme the germ of later themes and of subsequent developments. This single-theme or 'monothematic' principle gripped him throughout his life, and is the basis of many of the greatest movements in his symphonies and quartets. Here, as Ex. 7 shows, he is already working on these lines, and he does so repeatedly in the quartets of Op. 9 and Op. 17.

The other force at work in these quartets is the contrapuntal technique and texture that we saw him trying out in the vigorous two-part counterpoint of many of the minuets in his divertimento-quartets, and which he now handles with far greater confidence and mastery. How perfect a medium it was for controlling the *concertante* exuberance of his instruments and making all four parts sing is seen in the beautiful E minor trio in the

minuet of the E major Quartet, Op. 17, no. 1, which begins like
the echo of some motet in the polyphonic idiom from his days
as a cathedral choirboy:

Ex. 8

This vocal purity of line, once reconquered for his instrumental
music, was to be his throughout his life.

And if Haydn was attacking the problem of design in his first
movements along monothematic lines, he now brought his hard-
won contrapuntal mastery to bear on the problem of his finales.
To be exact, it was he who first began to see that there was a
problem there at all. As we observed earlier, the tradition in
which he grew up was of short, rapid, extremely light-weight
last movements. Such are his own early finales, and such, too,
even in Op. 9, is the curiously sketchy final *allegro* of no. 6 in A.
But he seems to have sensed at this point that a finale, in a work
of any substance, need not and should not be such a throw-away
affair, but should maintain the tension of the work to the end,
even if it were not to be the emotional climax, by means of wit
or craftsmanship, and so provide some sort of counterpoise
to the first movement. In the last movements of several early
symphonies he resorts to counterpoint as a means of giving them

solidity, and now he does the same for the emergent string quartet. In Op. 9, indeed, it is the finales in which the small-orchestra idiom of the early divertimenti survives most strongly. But in the splendid D minor, no. 4, the last movement owes much of its sinewy energy to the rhythmic impetus of its two-part contrapuntal opening, theme and counter-theme thrusting against each other. And how swiftly his mind is moving may be seen in a comparison of the last movements of Op. 9 with those of Op. 17, of which three (no. 2 in F, no. 3 in E flat, and no. 4 in C minor) have a strong element of linear and contra-puntal interest. This mental process reaches its logical conclusion in the three fugal final movements in the next set, Op. 20. Signifi-cantly, it is in these works where the linear, horizontal interest is strongest that the cello line moves most freely and actually, at times, lies highest; the phantom orchestral double-bass is rapidly fading out of Haydn's imagination.

In the quartets of Op. 9, the spacious, sonorous first movements of nos. 1 in C and 3 in G are of great distinction. No. 3, in addi-tion, is blessed with a crisp and witty finale, pure chamber-music albeit still in the divertimento tradition, and the noble serious-ness of its slow movement carries within itself the promise of still greater and more searching utterances. No. 2 in E flat has a particularly attractive minuet, on which Haydn also wrote a set of keyboard variations, and a dreamy recitative-and-aria type of slow movement in C minor, with a coda echoing the pathetic flute solo from the Elysian music in Gluck's *Orfeo*. The D minor, no. 4, touches real greatness. The tension and fire of the first movement, with its rhythmic foreshadowings of Mozart, are matched not only in the impetuous contrapuntal finale but also in the abrupt gestures and broken phrases of the minuet, to which the vocal polyphony of its little trio in the major provides an exquisite contrast. It is written as a trio (in the original, literal sense) for the two violins – not a contradiction in terms, for the first plays in double-stopping throughout.

With Op. 17, Haydn both expands his scale and consolidates and unifies his structure. A great German scholar, Friedrich Blume, has observed that in the quartets of Op. 17 the unity of all four movements, thematic and spiritual, is far closer than in Op. 9, and that in the first movements, the process of 'develop-ing' the principal themes is not confined to the middle section, traditionally called the development, but that they begin to develop from the moment of their inception, and go on doing so throughout the movement, right into the recapitulation. To illustrate this properly would require pages of music-type. All that is possible here is to ask the listener to follow the fortunes of the opening phrase of the F major, no. 2, throughout the first movement.

Ex. 9

In this gracious Quartet the serene minuet shows the same closely woven unity of theme and texture, heightened by the freedom and continuity of its long, irregular phrase-lengths. The first movement of the warm-hearted no. 1 in E major is derived no less closely from its opening theme; this is especially notice-able at the beginning of the development section and in the long cello passage towards the end of it. In subsequent movements Haydn makes telling use of the tonic minor (E minor), both in the singing, contrapuntal trio already quoted (Ex. 8 above) and in the dreamy lilt of the slow movement. In no. 3, in E flat, Haydn carries his urge towards integration to the length of deriving his first movement (a set of variations), minuet and finale from the same basic thematic idea. The minuet is a par-ticularly striking one, alike in its quirky, original themes, their overlapping imitative treatment, and in the remarkable scoring of the trio, second violin and cello singing the tune in octaves above and below a long held B flat on the viola to an undulating accompaniment on the first violin.

The C minor, no. 4, is perhaps the finest of the set, and certainly the most powerful. The first movement is a wonderful instance of the use of a single theme – here, the mere three notes of the opening phrase – not only to pervade and unify the entire movement but also, as a pivot, to swing the music round into different keys in the course of it. The bold C major of the minuet provides a splendid contrast both to the foregoing movement and to its tense, syncopated trio in the tonic minor. After a rather over-long slow movement the finale, with its impassioned themes and taut contrapuntal touches, brings the work to a noble and wholly balanced and satisfying culmination.

The remaining quartets of the set, no. 5 in G and no. 6 in D, are lighter in temper, with delightfully witty last movements. The slow movement of the G major, however, is in the tonic minor, and cast in the form of an operatic recitative and arioso, with the first violin as singer; Haydn was steeped in opera, and this expressive free declamation, with or without words, came naturally to him. So it did to Beethoven when, at a crucial point in the final movement of the Ninth Symphony, he reached out to seize upon the same resource; but that was to give utterance to an intenser and, at that juncture, almost prophetic vision.

The sequence culminates in the six masterpieces of Op. 20. Here the string quartet texture is finally achieved, however capable it may still be of further refinement or expansion. This is manifested, from the outset, in the complete emancipation of the cello, as we hear its deep-throated comment on the violin's opening statement in the first movement of no. 1 in E flat, or as it sings out exultantly in its tenor register with the main theme of no. 2 in C. But still more important is the way in which it brings its distinctive range of tone-qualities to that fusion of all four strings which is the essence of the string quartet, as it does in the richly modulating development section of the same movement, or, with quieter concentration, in the first movement of no. 4 in D.

Ex. 10
Allegro di molto

In this wonderful series each work is individual and distinct, and reveals a different aspect of Haydn's musical personality. His expansive warmth, ardour and poetry shine out in the C major: in the richness of melody and rhythmic pattern in the first movement, in the passion behind the darkly imaginative operatic-scena-without-words which constitutes the *adagio* and in the quiet emergence of the minuet, hesitant and syncopated, from the shadows of its closing chords into C major once more. The last movement is a fugue, one of the three fugal finales of the set; the others belong to nos. 5 in F minor and 6 in A. Together they constitute the final, frontal attack in Haydn's campaign to master contrapuntal technique. And there is no doubt that their intent, concentrated discussion – kept *sotto voce* throughout until the *forte* of the last few bars – represents, in his development, a triumph for the equality and freedom of all four instruments. It is none the less significant that he wrote only one more string-quartet fugue, the finale of Op. 50, no. 4. The mastery thus gained was not to be exerted for its own sake and in isolation, but fused with the other techniques on which his mature art rests.

The D major, no. 4, is a worthy companion to no. 2 in the noble fire and *gravitas* of its first two movements; indeed, its first movement is structurally the finer of the two, for its development evolves more closely and organically out of the themes of the opening section. The meditative D minor theme and variations of the second movement culminate in an extended and moving coda, growing out of the simple restatement of the theme at the fourth variation. In the minuet, marked *allegretto alla zingarese*, and in the finale, the spring of folk-melody which Haydn, like Bartók or Vaughan Williams in our own day, loved and absorbed into his own idiom, gloriously overflows its banks, submerging the minuet rhythm in a welter of syncopations, and turning the finale into the most hilarious he has yet written.

With the G minor, no. 3, and the F minor, no 5., Haydn penetrates further into the darker and more tragic regions which he had begun to explore in the D minor and C minor works of Op. 9 and 17. In the F minor, intensity of emotion is matched by his already mature breadth and freedom of phrasing and his newly won mastery of the medium. So much can be seen from the contrast between the wonderful long curve of the opening theme and the terser and squarer but no less distinctive rhythm of the second theme in the major: from the growth of the development section from these themes, and from the way in which the powerful coda plunges into the darkness of remote modulations and emerges to rise to a last climax of passion through what is in effect a fresh development of the second theme. To the dark intensity of this movement and of the minuet that follows, the quiet F major of the trio brings relief; still more does the slow movement, a tender and dreamlike pastorale in 6/8 time. The final fugue, on the venerable contrapuntal formula on which Handel based the chorus 'And with His stripes' in *Messiah*, provides a conclusion in which subjective emotion gives place to a more impersonal and intellectual tension.

The G minor no. 3, handicapped, perhaps, by a melodious but over-long slow movement, has always been overshadowed by its greater sister. But it is a no less mature work and, in a way, a more forward-looking one, the abruptnesses and acerbities of its outer movements forming a direct link with the tough-fibred minor-mode works of Haydn's fifties. Indeed, the finale, with its touches of contrapuntal texture within a sonata-form framework, is nearer to Haydn's ultimate solution of the problem of last-movement structure than his formal fugues. Nor does it lack the emotional fire of the F minor, whether in the rising passion of the little recitative-like figure for violin on its recapitulation in the first movement, or in the piercing cry of the minuet, with its E flat major Trio welling up quietly from the waters of comfort.

Of the two remaining quartets, no. 6 in A is a sweet-natured comedy, with a delightful variety of textures in the first movement and the wittiest and gayest of the fugal finales, in which Haydn shows off his technique and his high spirits by standing the principal subject on its head. No. 1 in E flat is a very different matter. Reticent and intimate in its quiet speech, it springs from that central core of tranquillity that lies at the heart of Haydn's music. This is the spirit that shines out in the clear, singing lines of the first movement, in the lyrical flowering of its development section from the apparently neutral passage-work earlier in the movement, and in the freedom and warmth of the recapitulation, showing these themes in fresh lights and shadows. The trio of the minuet shows it in the gentle descent of the first violin melody to meet the steady ascending line of second violin and cello. But its essence is revealed in the still depths of the slow movement. Marked *affettuoso e sostenuto*, it needs the utmost calm and steadiness in performance (unhurried and un-misled by the 3/8 time-signature) to allow its quiet flow to trace out its pure and exquisitely concentrated sonata-form outline and to reveal the timeless quality within its small compass. There is quietness even in the humour of the finale, with its three-bar phrases, persistent syncopations and *pianissimo* ending, and a touch of poetry in the passage of shifting modulations leading back to the recapitulation.

III

THE STRING QUARTET ESTABLISHED
HAYDN'S OP. 33, 42, 50, 54, 55, AND 64

Nine years passed before Haydn wrote another set of string quartets. Such a gap, after the achievement represented by the Op. 20 quartets, is at first sight puzzling. But at least part of the explanation is provided by the enormous expansion of Haydn's duties in the opera house and marionette theatre at Esterháza. These had become Prince Nicholas's ruling passion, and it is now known that between 1775 and 1781 Haydn was responsible for the entire musical side of over fifty operatic productions, besides composing five operas of his own, not counting a bunch of puppet operas for the marionette theatre. Small wonder that a good many of the symphonies of these years show a tendency to fall back on successful formulas, and that he had no energy to spare for the composition of string quartets, for which there seemed to be no demand.

Nor would it be surprising if, after the creative crisis of the early 1770s, Haydn had undergone some reaction, some recession of energy. As for the passionate attachment that had sprung up between him and the lively young singer Luigia Polzelli, unhappily married like himself, whom the Prince had engaged in 1779, we cannot know if it was a stimulus or a distraction. But by 1780 the tide was beginning to turn. Power began to flow back into the symphonies composed about this time (among them *La Chasse*, no. 73, and the splendid no. 75 in D); and towards the end of 1781 we find him writing around to potential subscribers announcing the issue of six 'brand-new *à quadro* . . . written in a new and special way, for I have not composed any for ten years'. These are the set published in 1782 as Op. 33.

Various interpretations have been placed upon Haydn's description of these six quartets as being 'written in a new and special way'. Possibly, as some have suggested, Haydn is using the phrase as a selling-point. But at the same time it represents a consciousness on his part that in the architecture of the movements, in the treatment of the thematic material within the movement, in the handling of the instruments, both individually and as an integrated texture, everything that in Op. 20 wears an air of triumphant but strenuous endeavour has here become completely effortless. Nowhere is this effortless mastery more apparent than in the character of the themes themselves: not mere tunes but pregnant figures capable of organic growth and development, of carrying the weight of an extended structure while revealing themselves in fresh lights and shadows. The listener can verify this for himself by observing what happens to the main theme in the first movements of each of the first three quartets, and in particular to the figures marked ⌐x⌐ in the quotations given below.

Ex. 11 *(a)*

Allegro moderato

Op. 33
No. 1

No. 2

(b) Allegro moderato, cantabile

No. 3

(c) Allegro moderato

This close thematic unity throughout a movement cannot but affect the structure of the movement as a whole. Already in Op. 9 and Op. 17 we have seen Haydn beginning to treat the pattern of 'first-movement' or 'sonata' form monothematically, by introducing his principal theme, or a variant of it, into the second group of themes that appears when the music has moved away from the tonic to its new key-centre. Now, however, if he is going to base all his musical thinking on a single predominant theme, so that the entire first section grows out of it before it goes on to pervade the development, the recapitulation will run the risk of monotony. But his growing fascination with the possibilities of the monothematic movement goes hand in hand with an ever increasing freedom in his recapitulation sections. Sometimes he achieves a wonderfully varied and emotionally intensified recapitulation in a shorter space, telescoping the action at one point so that another phrase may be built up into a climax; this is his procedure in the first three quartets of Op. 33. In the last three – less closely monothematic, though the first and second groups of themes are rhythmically interlinked – he tries out for the first time a new and significant line in his recapitulations, expanding them into fresh contours and through new and often remote keys, so that they become virtually second developments. The first movement of no. 6 in D provides an admirable example: (1) shows the secondary theme which emerges from the principal subject as it first appears; (2) shows how it is deflected on recapitulation.

Ex. 12

In this set the minuet movements are all entitled 'scherzo' or 'scherzando' (and marked *allegro* or *allegretto*). The application of this term to the minuet is, at this point, simply a designation of lightness and gaiety and an indication that Haydn is working within the faster of the two minuet tempi; the one-in-a-bar scherzo still lies in the future. But the tremendous forward urge in the scherzando of the B minor, no. 1, and the comical displaced accents in the scherzo of no. 5 foreshadow things to come.

In these quartets Haydn is still at grips with the problem of the last movement; but here, as if realizing that the fugal finales of Op. 20 went too far in the direction of intellectuality, he swings over to the other extreme, and in three out of these six (nos. 2, 3 and 4) the finales are in simple rondo form and as hilariously funny as he can make them. That the last two quartets of the set have variation finales may perhaps suggest that he was not satisfied with this solution either. But he held all the clues in his hands, sonata and rondo forms and contrapuntal textures, and the next ten years were to see him achieve, in quartet and symphony alike, the immensely satisfying synthesis represented by his ripest last movements.

It is no accident that Haydn should have written his most closely organized and emotionally tense finale, the only one of the set in sonata form, to the B minor Quartet, no. 1. From Op. 9 on, each set contains its minor-mode work, rising to tragic passion in the quartets of his late thirties. Now, at fifty, the tragic vision has left him. In its place we find a harder, more intellectual passion touched with irony, a quality we recognize at once in Beethoven, and which should no longer surprise us in Haydn once we recognize it for what it is. This B minor Quartet is full of it, right from the opening bars, with their ambiguous tonality poised between B minor and D major; it even touches the *andante*, with its pungent chromaticisms, carried out with all the boldness of Haydn's octave writing between pairs of strings.

No. 2 in E flat is a less closely unified work, moving as it does on two emotional levels. Its first and slow movements share the inward and meditative spirit of Op. 20, no. 1, in the same key, the *largo sostenuto* showing Haydn's two-part writing used, not in bold *al fresco* style but for line-drawing of the purity and simplicity of Giotto's O. This is counterpoint of as high an order as any formal fugue, and Haydn carries its resources with him into his latest works. The scherzo-minuet is square-cut, turning to frank rusticity in the *Ländler*-like trio, and the galloping rondo-finale ends with the famous 'Joke' (a nickname sometimes given to this Quartet), in which the main theme returns with protracted pauses between its phrases, to trick the listener into thinking the music is over. No. 3 in C ('The Bird') is once more a perfect unity, radiating joy from the opening notes of the first movement, so spontaneous yet so completely integrated, to its glorious rondo-finale based on a Slavonic dance tune. Its crowning marvel is the grave and tender scherzo, all the instruments on their lowest string; nowhere else, perhaps, in all music does C major sound so dark. The trio brings back bird-song with its airy duet between the two violins. The Papageno-ish no. 4 in B flat and no. 5 in G are altogether lighter, but their first movements explore boldly and brilliantly the possibilities of a very free and extended recapitulation, and the scherzo of the G major is a delicious piece of rhythmic fooling. No. 6 in D shows its serious side in its grave and beautiful D minor *andante* and in the quiet grace of its concluding variations. These are the first example in Haydn's quartets of that double variation pattern, alternating major and minor, which he himself devised and in which he cast some of his greatest movements, albeit chiefly in his symphonies and keyboard works, and which, in Beethoven's hands, was to reveal still vaster potentialities.

One can perhaps put one's finger upon the years immediately following the appearance of the Op. 33 quartets as the point at which the string quartet, as such, became finally and universally recognized as a medium and genre of composition; for, while the eighteen quartets of Haydn's Op. 9, 17 and 20 had brought it into being, and had been working like a ferment among discerning musical minds in the intervening years, the Op. 33 quartets, appearing with all the force of Haydn's by now considerable reputation behind them, attracted far more attention. And in one quarter their effect was catalytic. As a lad of sixteen Mozart had already felt the impact of the Op. 20 set and reflected it in the contrapuntal textures of the early quartets K.168 to 173; two of them even have fugal finales. Now, in 1782, Mozart arrived in Vienna to launch out on his precarious freelance career just as the Op. 33 set appeared. His immediate reaction was to start writing string quartets again himself. The G major, K.387, was composed in that same year, and was the first of the great set of six, written over the next few years, which he published with a prefatory letter of dedication to Haydn, full of touching humility and affection. Mozart had first met Haydn, twenty-four years his senior, in 1781, but the meeting had been brief, and Haydn's rare visits to Vienna gave little opportunity for the friendship to ripen. But during the winter season of 1784–5 Prince Nicholas Esterházy and his suite spent longer than usual in the Imperial capital, thus making it possible for Haydn to pursue the acquaintanceship with visits and quartet parties at Mozart's home and in the company of their friends. It was at one such party, in February 1785, that the newly composed A major and C major Quartets from Mozart's 'Haydn' set were played in the presence of Mozart's father, who wrote home to his daughter in Salzburg that Haydn had said to him, 'I tell you before God, as an honest man, that your son is the greatest composer I know, either personally or by name; he has taste, and moreover the greatest science in composition'.

From now on, the ferment of Mozart's influence was at work in Haydn. In these quartets which his own genius had fathered, Haydn's generous, receptive and still resilient mind and heart recognized his own art and medium carried to a still higher level of technical mastery and expressive intensity than he himself had attained. The assimilation of this new influence, whether by absorbing features of Mozart's style or by the unfolding of resources implicit but still only partially developed in his own art, did not come about all at once; Haydn's life and development moved in a slower rhythm than Mozart's. And in the London symphonies and in the Masses and quartets of the late 1790s we can still see the working of the influence that had touched his being so profoundly in the previous decade.

In the six years before the publication of the next set of quartets in 1787 Haydn's increasing fame brought him commissions from many quarters: publishers in Vienna and London, aristocratic music-lovers from German principalities, concert-giving organizations like the *Concert spirituel* in Paris, for which he wrote the six Paris symphonies. Then, from remote Cadiz, the Cathedral Chapter wrote in 1786 asking for a sequence of orchestral interludes to be played in the course of a Good Friday service of meditations on the Seven Words from the Cross. This work, which Haydn himself subsequently arranged for string quartet (and later, again, as a choral work) made a profound impression, not least on Haydn himself. To him, it represented a challenge and a problem; as he himself put it, 'the task of writing seven *adagios* . . . to preserve a connection between them without wearying the hearers, was none of the lightest'. Thus, the solution put forward by a priest friend, that he should let the Latin text of each of Our Lord's utterances suggest to him a musical theme on which to base his successive movements, was providential, for the evolving of an entire movement from a single theme was already second nature to him. In the *Seven Words* the music is monothematic both spiritually and musically, and the concentration and unity here achieved were to be reflected in all his subsequent composition.

This is immediately apparent in the next set of quartets, published in 1787 and dedicated to King Frederick William II

33

of Prussia, a curious personality but a good cellist and enthusiastic patron of the arts. (Mozart also wrote three quartets for him.) But before that we find, isolated and mysterious, the little D minor Quartet of which the autograph is dated 1785 and which was subsequently labelled Op. 42. Nothing is known about its background and origin, save perhaps a passing reference in one of Haydn's letters to three 'very short' quartets 'intended for Spain'; but no others have survived. Its brevity and simplicity have puzzled critics and historians; Marion Scott made the imaginative suggestion that it was designed for a group of possibly youthful beginners, since the second-violin part does not go above the second position. But this brevity and simplicity are those of complete mastery. The first movement might be described as a Young Person's Guide to monothematic sonata-form construction, evolving, with tranquil lucidity, entirely from the two main motives of its first subject. The finale spells out with the same clarity and simplicity how to compose a fugal movement in sonata form, and the *adagio*, unfolding peacefully from its opening phrase, is one of Haydn's most intimate and light-filled meditations.

In the quartets of Op. 50, a richly varied group in character and emotion, the possibilities of monothematic first-movement structure are explored powerfully, persistently and in a number of directions. In the first of the set, in B flat, Haydn approaches the matter with calm concentration and a certain emotional detachment. The first movement is so closely woven from its initial phrases that a single quotation of the opening bars shows the melodic and rhythmic basis of the entire movement: the repeated crotchets, the little theme (*a*) and its rhythmic transformation into triplets.

Ex. 13

The first movement of no. 3 in E flat is again closely derived from its opening phrases, with a touch of linear counterpoint in the variant of the main theme which serves as second subject; this is further exploited in the development, and gives the beautifully free and allusive little movement its almost mathematical elegance. In both works the last movements are monothematic too. In no. 1, the brilliantly funny and high-spirited finale carries its opening theme, right way up, upside down, whole, in fragments and in combination with others, through all the ins and outs of a free and complex rondo-like pattern. The finale of the E flat, no. 3, is even more closely concentrated, completely absorbed in the pursuit of its opening theme through all the modulations of a perfectly planned sonata-form movement.

The graceful set of variations which forms the slow movement of the B flat Quartet is the first to follow a design which Haydn was to find increasingly rich in inspiration, alike in symphonies and quartets – one containing a single variation in the minor, treated with considerable freedom in relation to the theme. Once this idea had lodged in Haydn's mind he was quick to follow it up in the *andante più tosto allegretto* of no. 3, a little jewel of a movement, opening with one of his most finely drawn pieces of two-part harmony and treating the *minore* variation as a wonderfully free commentary on the first four notes of the theme.

The D major Quartet, no. 6 of the set ('The Frog'), is a splendid work in which monothematic concentration is placed at the service of a strong emotional warmth and urgency in both first movement and finale. The latter is permeated by its initial motive of reiterated semiquavers produced by playing the same notes alternately on neighbouring strings, an effect sufficiently suggestive of the croaking of a frog to earn the quartet its nickname. The deeply felt slow movement is in D minor, its emotional utterance intensified by its sudden plunges into remote keys.

The remaining three quartets, different as they are in personality, share the same thematic concentration. Of their first movements only that of no. 2 in C cannot properly be called monothematic, since it possesses a distinct and tuneful group of second subjects. But the structural weight is borne by the opening theme, both in the development section proper and in the recapitulation, which Haydn tightens into a fresh development by treating the theme in canon, right way up and upside down. Here is a superb instance of the use of technical virtuosity for architectural ends. The sunny and seemingly artless F major, no. 5, demonstrates that it is possible for a beautifully free and subtle first movement to evolve out of a couple of cadential formulae, and its *poco adagio* (sometimes called 'The Dream') is a singularly lovely example of a type of slow movement found in Haydn's music from the F minor Quartet of Op. 20 to the London symphonies, in which delicate figuration drifts gently around a slow, almost trance-like basic pulse.

The first movement of the F sharp minor Quartet, no. 4, gets the best of both worlds, because the principal theme, appearing n the major where the second-subject group should be, achieves an effect of contrast as well as unity. But it is in fact as closely monothematic as any in this set, and its immense driving energy is due to the continual thrust of Haydn's characteristic rhythm (cf. Ex. 2), appearing as ♫♩ and as ♫♩♪ . The *andante* is a set of variations on alternating themes, the A major sweetness of the first theme a perfect foil to the sombre depths of sound and harmonic asperity of the second in the minor; and the last movement is a wonderful fusion of fugal treatment and sonata-form design, in which the subject is developed organically and with cumulative passion and power.

In all three quartets, thematic unity is even carried over into the minuets, for minuet and trio are thematically linked. In the C major, no. 2, the link is more in the pattern of the themes, •stalking up and down the notes of successive major and minor chords, than in the actual melody. But in the wonderfully unified minuet of no. 5 in F, theme and rhythm are carried over into the F minor trio, which, with its free and flexible phrase-groupings,

36

makes a remarkable extended development of the minuet itself. The most striking of the three, perhaps, is the minuet of the F sharp minor. It is in the major, moving and modulating with immense energy on a rhythm which carries over into the austerely contrapuntal trio in the minor, thus providing a powerful unity as well as strong contrast.

Between 1788 and 1790 Haydn wrote twelve quartets for Johann Tost, a violinist in Prince Nicholas Esterházy's orchestra, who after touring abroad in 1789 left the musical profession, married a lady in the Prince's household, and became a prosperous merchant. These quartets fall into two sets of six. The first, published in two batches of three each as Op. 54 and Op. 55, were probably composed in 1788; the second set was composed in 1790 and published as Op. 64. Understandably, the first violin part is prominent throughout the two sets, sometimes even to the point of transgressing against that equality and integration which Haydn's own quartets had made the essence of true quartet writing. But more often it is used as an artistic resource, calling for technical virtuosity from the first violin to lend fire and eloquence to the music. This is outstandingly the case in the powerful and original C major Quartet, Op. 54, no. 2: in the first movement, with its bold, striding gestures and big sonorities, and in the C minor *adagio*, in which the first violin breaks into impassioned arabesques above the dark and brooding melody, in the manner of a wild Hungarian lament. (The nearest parallel in classical chamber music is the minor section in the slow movement of Brahms's Clarinet Quintet.) The minuet, which follows without break, has a powerful trio also in the tonic minor. In fact this work would rank with the greatest of Haydn's but that the finale is somehow out of balance, whether one sees it as a slow movement with a *presto* episode, or a tiny *presto* with an over-weighted slow introduction recurring at the end. This is the more tantalizing in view of the quality of the rest of the work. Floridity runs to seed in the slow movement of Op. 54, no. 3, in E major, otherwise a fine and warm-hearted work in which the themes of the first and last movements are inspired in themselves and treated with splendid imagination and consistency. The outer movements of no. 1 in G are rhythmically lively but somewhat prosaic, but there is real poetry in the *allegretto*, with its remote modulations, foreshadowing Schubert.

In the Op. 55 set Haydn reinforces his sensitiveness to the range of possible harmonies to a given phrase by the addition of Mozartean chromaticism. The first movement and minuet of the lovely and little-known no. 3 in B flat are full of it, in melody and harmony, and there are touches in the whirling final *presto* in which we seem to catch glimpses of Zerlina's mischievous face. But the different harmonic colours given to the first subject in the course of the first movement are essential Haydn; so, too, are the variations that constitute the slow movement, with their grave and candid sweetness and underlying march-like tread, most marked when the final, very free variation treats the theme, contrapuntally, in an unorthodox but curiously moving canon. The *adagio* of no. 1 in A is a sister movement, hardly less beautiful: a rondo, scored with warm sonority, its second episode in the minor breaking into closely interlocking lines of counterpoint; after the final return of the main theme, at the point where, in his earlier days, Haydn would have allowed a virtuoso first violinist to improvise a cadenza, there is a rich and imaginative written-out cadenza for all four instruments. The captivating trio of the minuet exploits the upper register of Tost's violin with piquant and wholly legitimate effect, and the rondo-finale is given body and cohesion by its sparkling fugal episode; the final return of the main theme is iridescent with the new harmonic colours with which Haydn touches the opening phrase.

But if there are touches of Mozart's influence in these two quartets, Haydn's individuality is stamped on the F minor, no. 2, from beginning to end. (Its nickname, the 'Razor', springs from the doubtful legend that he gave it to a visiting London publisher in exchange for an English razor.) The slow movement comes first, a set of alternating minor-major variations. The minor theme, with its astringent harmonies, is one of Haydn's most characteristic and personal. No less characteristic is the soaring sweetness of the alternating theme in F major, but here the emphasis laid on the first violin condemns the lower parts to dullness, until, in the final variation, the cello sweeps in, in its tenor register, to steal the show. The *allegro* that follows concentrates sternly on its prickly theme, with its oddly inflected intervals and abrupt rhythms, through minor and major and a network of keys and contrapuntal textures in the development: a wonderful piece of musical rebarbativeness which would surprise no one in the context of a Beethoven quartet. In total contrast, there is a strange inwardness about the minuet, with its quiet reiterations of the theme by one instrument after another. This touch of withdrawnness and mystery, a quality always latent in Haydn, is one which was to grow on him in his final years. The last movement is in the major, but its chromaticisms, Mozartean though they may be in origin, lend its gaiety a wholly Haydnish edge.

The year 1790 was one of kaleidoscopic changes for Haydn. In January he was in Vienna, attending the rehearsals of the first production of *Così fan tutte* in Mozart's company and welcomed and made much of among his circle of friends. His happiest relationship was with the Genzinger family, in whose home he was a constant visitor, coaching the children in singing, and composing keyboard works for their gifted and charming mother, Maria Anna. In February he was back in Esterhàza, reluctant and depressed, and at the end of the month Prince Nicholas's wife died. Inconsolable, the Prince kept Haydn constantly at his side in incessant and increasingly wearing duties, and throughout the spring and summer Haydn poured out his loneliness and frustration in his letters to Maria Anna von Genzinger, to whom he wrote more freely than to anyone else in his life. This was the background of events against which he wrote his second set of quartets for Johann Tost, those published as Op. 64. Perhaps the stimulus came from the lady who had become Prince Nicholas's housekeeper after his wife's death, Maria Anna von Jerlischek, the 'Fräulein Nanette' of Haydn's letters, whom Tost subsequently married.

Although the quartets of Op. 64 are still weighted in favour of the first violin, they bring so much interest and variety to the other parts, and so much sheer beauty of sound to delight players and listeners alike, as to make ample amends. And in their freedom and mastery of design and of thematic development they maintain a consistently high level. The only exception is no. 1 in C, which somehow never takes wing; yet even here the first movement, with its bold and freely modulating recapitulation, shows Haydn's sense of structure and key at its most adventurous. If, in discussing the other five quartets of the set, emphasis is laid on the first movements, it is because they are splendidly representative of the character and range of Haydn's mature musical architecture as he drew near, though he did not know it, to the end of an epoch in his life.

The B minor Quartet, no. 2 of the set, concentrates within itself all the characteristics of Haydn's minor-mode works, beginning with the ambiguous tonality of the principal theme, which, as stated at the outset, by the first violin alone, could be major or minor until the other instruments enter to drive it on to its minor cadence.

Ex. 14

This theme, especially the four-note figure marked *a*, is the key to the melodic and rhythmic life of the movement. But there are other themes of vital importance: the little descending chromatic figure on the rhythm of *a*, the cluster of dancing tunes in D major cut short by a sudden furious plunge into D minor, and the ensuing ominous unison theme – in minims, on a rising sixth moving chromatically upwards – which stalks into the development in octaves, and into which the recapitulation finally storms on a mounting tide of fury, its intervals now stretched to towering double octaves – a climax of astonishing power. The B major of the ensuing *adagio*, a set of continuously linked variations, shines out all the more radiantly after this dark and angry close. The minuet, with its biting reiterated ♩ ♫ ♩ rhythm, is a sardonic scherzo in spirit if not in name or (quite yet) in speed, with another brilliant B major contrast in the lyrical trio, and the *presto* finale is concentratedly monothematic, from beginning to major end, evolving entirely from the rhythm of its opening theme.

In the witty first movement of no. 3 in B flat, with its first subject a pattern of dancing rhythms, Haydn appears to abandon monothematic principles and satisfy all canons of orthodoxy by producing an admirably contrasted second subject, in smooth lyrical vein, and then featuring it in the minor in the development. But in his recapitulation he tightens up the whole movement by cutting out this lyrical theme and concentrating entirely on the dancing rhythms, from their hesitant return, balanced irresolutely between G minor and the original B flat, to their final tiptoe exit. Rhythm again carries all before it in the irresistible minuet, with its cross-accents and syncopated trio, making delectable play with the same idea Haydn had tried out so happily in the *Oxford* Symphony the year before. These syncopations are carried over into the last movement, a cheerfully animated rondo-cum-sonata-form affair clouding over at intervals into hushed, brooding passages of sustained minims. Such passages of long, held notes recur frequently in Haydn's mature *allegro* movements – as we see in his quartets from Op. 17 onwards – and are perhaps characteristic of a mind for which even meditation could sometimes be an explosive process.

With no. 4, in G, Haydn shows once again that he can carry over into movements with two distinct and recognizable groups of themes that close unity combined with extreme freedom of design which marks his purely monothematic movements. Here his group of second subjects has three distinct members – a fresh version of the first subject, a syncopated tune in the minor, and a warm, dark, song-like tune played, almost as an afterthought, by the first violin on his lowest string. The development, focused on the second-subject tunes, is short; but in the recapitulation the first subject has hardly returned before it swings away into a new key and what is virtually a fresh development, in which the familiar themes are shaped into new contours without losing their recognizable identity. The minuet is a fresh and delightful example of his rustic *Ländler* dances, and the finale a hilarious 6/8 *galop*, shooting off at the most capricious harmonic tangents in its middle section.

Perhaps the most boldly original as well as the most beautiful of them all is the first movement of no. 5 in D. There are, beside the singing, soaring first-violin melody which has earned for this quartet its nickname 'The Lark', two other themes of vital importance; the sharply syncopated, sharply modulating theme which thrusts the music decisively away from the home key and

41

on to A major, and the cascade of triplets followed by a chromatic ascent which does duty for a second subject.

Ex.15

Allegro moderato

Syncopations and triplets alike figure largely in the development, and after the return of the first theme in the recapitulation, there is a wonderful further expansion of the second subject, Ex. 15, rising in glowing colours to its climax, followed by the most surprising stroke of all as the first subject sails in again and starts a brand-new recapitulation. Nowhere else does Haydn achieve quite the same effect of spaciousness and freedom combined with thematic concentration. Also remarkable in this quartet is the ghostly, chromatic minor trio of the minuet, in which he seems to hark back to the practice and spirit of his earliest works, and the dash and sparkle of the non-stop final *presto*, scampering in and out of its fugal middle section with breathtaking speed and *élan*.

In no. 6 in E flat Haydn returns to a true monothematic first movement. Quiet and thoughtful, like all his works in that key, and less dramatic in its beauty than the D major, it is even finer in the close polyphonic interweaving of its parts around the principal theme in the development, and in the Beethovenish modulating passage which he builds up on its tiny cadential closing figure. The final rondo, like that of no. 5, is full of good fuguing, but the most perfect part-writing is reserved for the *andante*, with its melodic lines serenely curving and intersecting in tender dissonances.

IV

BETWEEN TWO EPOCHS
OP. 71, OP. 74

In September 1790 Prince Nicholas Esterházy died. Less than three months later, Haydn was on his way across Europe, with the violinist Salomon, heading for London. Salomon had been trying for years unsuccessfully to secure Haydn for a London season, and the death of Prince Nicholas, releasing Haydn from the bonds of duty and affection that bound him to his old master, gave him his chance; for the new Prince, who did not care for music, had dismissed most of the orchestra, retaining Haydn on full pay but with purely nominal duties. To Haydn, Salomon's offer brought the longed for opportunity for a complete break. Cheerfully disregarding the advice of friends, including Mozart, who thought him too old at fifty-eight for such a venture, he made the decision which was to bring him not only fame and friendships and an honorary doctorate from Oxford University, but also the exhilaration and the challenge of a new world: the world of London music, with its crowded concert rooms, its eager, enthusiastic audiences, its busy intrigue and competition behind the scenes. All this he met with a superb uprush of vitality and zest which carried him through the physical strain of living and working under constant pressure, and in the process released the still untapped springs of creative life within him.

He returned home in the summer of 1792 and settled down in Vienna to a round of light duties for his new master Prince Anton Esterházy, composing, and teaching a few pupils, among them the twenty-two-year-old Beethoven. Life in Vienna had, however, lost much of its old charm for him, since Mozart had died during his absence, and early in 1793 came a fresh grief with the death of Maria Anna von Genzinger, whom he had so eagerly looked forward to seeing again on his return. This was the year in which he composed the wonderful F minor piano Variations and the six quartets which subsequently appeared in two sets as Op. 71 and Op. 74, dedicated to Count Anton Apponyi, whose family was connected by marriage with the Esterházys. He also composed the Symphony in E flat, no. 99, probably with a view to a second London visit, which in fact took place in 1794 and from which he returned, never to travel abroad again, in 1795.

The six 'Apponyi' quartets are separated by the watersheds of the two English visits, on the one hand, from the twenty-five quartets of his life at Esterháza in the 1780s and, on the other, from the eight which he wrote after his final homecoming. Thus they stand poised between two epochs. Theirs is the profound fascination of all transitional works in which a living creative mind is at work gathering up past achievements, struggling to assimilate recent experiences, reaching out towards new perceptions and new ways of expressing them: and, in Haydn's case, beginning to reflect the changing perspectives that come with approaching age.

It is in their scoring that the effort and struggle of this process of transition is most evident, and it may well be, as many believe, that the experience of the powerful and accomplished London orchestras (considerably larger than the Esterháza ensemble) here drove Haydn to stretch his quartet style beyond the limits of the medium in quest of fuller, almost orchestral sonorities. The great leaping octaves of the first movement of Op. 71, no. 2, in D spring to mind here as the most obvious instance; and there are passages in which, for the first time for many years, the viola crosses the cello in such a way that a double bass is needed to restore the true bass of the harmony. Experienced chamber-music players also point to 'movements in which it is perplexing to find a tempo that will exactly fit, a speed that would be satisfactory enough on the orchestral strings being unsatisfactory at one point or other on the string quartet'.[1] Elsewhere, the richer sonority which Haydn is striving after is fully attained, as in the clarity and depth of the first movement and minuet of the C major, Op. 74, no. 1, and carried over into the works of his latest period.

But there are other, almost opposing tendencies which foreshadow the future no less strongly. There are movements in which the texture takes on an increasingly spare, linear quality – quite apart from the constant recurrence of passages in fugal or imitative counterpoint – and Haydn returns repeatedly and purposefully to the bold, bare octave writing of his early days.

[1] Athol Page, *Playing String Quartets* (Longman, 1964), p. 57.

Yet another foreshadowing of his final maturity is the intensification of his feeling for the mystery and strangeness of the remoter keys, chiefly manifested, in this group of quartets, by his laying them alongside each other as a simple contrast between two strong, pure colours, as in the trios of the minuets of the C major and F major, Op. 74, nos. 1 and 2. Structurally he was becoming even more strongly monothematic and more incalculable, and he began to devise new forms as well as treating the old with greater freedom and concentration.

All six works begin with short introductions: sometimes a mere sequence of chords, sometimes a more extended passage. The first movement of the B flat Quartet, Op. 71, no. 1, is perhaps a little low in voltage, despite its easy yet compact monothematic evolution. But the *adagio* is an exquisite instance of Haydn speaking Mozart's musical language in his own completely personal way, using remote, almost abrupt modulations with the tenderest expressiveness. The varied harmonizations of the main tune give depth and colour to the minuet, and the finale is a gay and completely unclassifiable rondo-like creature, conjuring up a peasant dance to the bagpipes in the course of a long concatenation of 'second subjects'.

The D major Quartet, Op. 71, no. 2, is the most orchestral in aspiration, with its *adagio* introduction in the manner of a symphonic first movement leading into the angular octave leaps and rushing semiquavers of the *allegro*. All this undoubtedly produces a sense of strain; but there is a visionary quality about it none the less, and when, at the recapitulation, and again in the coda, the leaping octaves thrust upwards through new and distant harmonies, it is as if Haydn were pushing open a door through which Beethoven was to pass. Deep, remote modulations and undulating semiquaver figuration intensify the dreamlike quality of the *adagio*; by contrast the minuet, and still more the trio, are fined down to the laconic spareness characteristic of Haydn in his more withdrawn utterances. Only the finale is beneath the level of this powerful and problematical work – a too easy rondo on a too easy-going tune; yet even here he is feeling his way towards something new in the sudden change of speed from *allegretto* to *allegro*, foreshadowing an idea which he brought to fulfilment in the first movements of two great quartets in Op. 76.

It is in the third quartet, in E flat, that the spareness of line and the withdrawn, inward gaze are most strongly marked: in the first movement, intently and tersely monothematic; in the theme of the *andante* – a set of variations – with its edged harmonies, and the wonderful veiled darkness of the two minor variations; in the close concentration of the minuet on its theme, and the chromatic inflections of the trio; and in the completely original, completely monothematic finale, with its tracts of two-part octave writing.

The first movement of the C major, Op. 74, no. 1, is a masterpiece of design, monothematic with a very free recapitulation, which, by treating the principal theme in canon, produces a marvellous effect of expansion within the same space. Its *andantino grazioso* is another piece of Mozartean diction transmuted into essential Haydn; here the two-part octave writing gives the music an inimitable blend of delicacy and toughness. The trio of the minuet shines out with all the brightness of its contrasting key, A major, a contrast that may obscure the fact that its theme and that of the minuet are variants of each other. The finale is a free and brilliant sonata-form movement, with a sequence of rustic dance-tunes – like Op. 71, no. 1, and again over a bagpipe drone – for a second subject: another anticipation of the last quartets.

The F major, Op. 74, no. 2, is the lightest of the six in temper; perhaps a little the less interesting for posing no problems, but brilliant in its scoring, especially in the delicious *andante* variations, and touching romantic depths in the dark D flat major into which the trio pivots from the minuet. The finale delights us by its comical contrast between the featherweight tune and the faintly pompous contrapuntal tag with which it is fugally combined in the development, but it is where the contrapuntal skill is least conspicuous that it is at its most masterly, especially in the close canonic overlappings of the main tune.

The G minor, no. 3, nicknamed 'The Rider' on account of its galloping rhythms, is the best known of the quartets in this group. Its outer movements are carried along by a driving energy which, in the first movement, catches up the introductory bars and absorbs them into the fabric of the main part of the movement. In the minuet, and still more in the shifting modulations of the trio, this energy is suffused with poetry. But it is in the noble *largo assai* (its key, E major, in luminous contrast with the G major ending of the first movement) that Haydn reaches forward, more than anywhere else in the work, to the depth of vision which he attained in his final years.

V

THE FINAL MATURITY
OP. 76, OP. 77, OP. 103

Haydn returned from England in 1795 to the service of his fourth master of the Esterházy family, Prince Nicholas II, an unsympathetic personality but a considerable patron of the arts. The Prince had virtually abandoned Esterháza and fixed his residence at the palace at Eisenstadt, the ancestral home of his family, spending his winters in the capital. Haydn's time was thus divided between Vienna and the quiet little town where he had come to take up his duties as a young man. Here the Prince maintained his musical establishment, but Haydn's duties were lighter than of old, the chief of them being the composition and performance, each September, of a Mass for the name-day of the Princess, who was a true friend to Haydn and as warm-hearted as her husband was unbending. Thus the palace chapel at Eisenstadt witnessed the first performance of the six great Masses which Haydn composed between 1796 and 1802. But he had returned from London fired by Handel's music to attempt an oratorio himself; and it was in Vienna that the triumphant first performance of *The Creation* took place in 1798.

It was probably some time in 1796 that Count Joseph Erdödy commissioned six string quartets from Haydn, for by the summer of 1797 he was already playing them through on the piano to visitors. They were published in 1799 as Op. 76. In that year he received a fresh commission for six quartets from Prince Lobkowitz, Beethoven's patron. He completed two that year – later published as Op. 77 – besides composing the lovely 'Theresa' Mass and embarking on *The Seasons*, of which he also completed 'Spring'. But *The Seasons*, which he had been persuaded to undertake against his will, drained his vitality. He finished the work by 1801, and wrote two more magnificent Masses, but was unable to complete the set of quartets. All he had the strength to write were the two middle movements, *andante* and minuet, of a projected Quartet in D minor. These were eventually published as his 'Last Quartet'.

But the eight quartets which he completed show no sign of flagging powers. And in that last great wave of energy which carried them to completion he gathers up all the efforts and conquests, all the explorations, all the personal idiosyncrasies too, of nearly half a century of unbroken creative life. Nowhere is his thematic and structural concentration so powerful, his contrapuntal writing so strong and closely woven, his ranging through the furthest reaches of key so searching and profound. If elsewhere some of his best instrumental finales are based upon folksongs and dances, here he even surpasses them in exhilaration and closeness of texture. The two-part writing which had always been a habit and resource now reveals its full potentialities and contrasts, whether for orchestral harshness or lyrical vocal intimacy, dancing lightness or profound meditation. The phrase structure is endlessly varied and flexible, now square and symmetrical, now unfolding in long, continuous paragraphs, according to the character and inner life of the themes themselves. And behind this and permeating it all is a quality hard to define, but one in which we can sense the weight of a lifetime's experience, human and musical. No young mind and heart could have conceived this music, could so have tempered exuberance with gentleness, or touched sober steadfastness with vision.

The first quartet of the Op. 76 set, in G, seems to be turning back, almost deliberately, to consolidate the ground newly gained. The first movement is the quintessence of Haydn's string writing at its most vocal, building up from the quiet, easygoing tune sung at the outset by the cello alone, answered by the viola, then moving into two parts, then into four, before they suddenly crystallize into a string quartet again. The entire movement is poised between the sonorities of the string quartet and this wonderfully clear and fine-drawn vocal counterpoint. The *adagio* that follows takes up the burden of the great song sung in the slow movement of the 'Rider' Quartet and carries it further, with a richer design (a very free rondo), more profound and questing modulations in the minor episodes, and a greater range of string-quartet scoring. The so-called minuet belongs indeed to two epochs, for the principal section is marked *presto:* and is a one-in-a-bar scherzo in all but name, whereas the trio, with its easier-paced slurred quavers, belongs unmistakably to the family of Haydn's peasant *Ländler*, whether in the quartets or in the Paris and London symphonies. The finale again shows its kinship with the 'Rider' Quartet in its hurtling rhythm and in its key-structure, beginning in the tonic minor and emerging finally into the major in the recapitulation; but this design is more striking in a work in the major mode, and the perpetual triplet rhythm gives it a closer unity and intensifies the impact of the brief moments in which the music is stilled into solemnity. The triplet rhythm even underlies the deliciously insouciant new tune, apparently irrelevant but in fact derived from the main theme, which dances in, over a pizzicato accompaniment, at the very end of the movement.

The first movement in the D minor, no. 2, ranks with Haydn's most concentrated passages of musical thinking, for it is all focused on the motive of falling fifths heard at the outset on the first violin and which bears the entire movement through all its orbit of key changes, all its expressive range and contrasts of scoring. If the graceful and subtly organized D major *andante* that follows leaves a faint sense of disappointment, it is only because one feels it to be a little too light in temper for its formidable context, for the next movement is the famous so-called 'Witches' Minuet', in canon, throughout its sinewy length, between upper and lower strings. Here is the superbly logical fulfilment of the two-part octave doubling of Haydn's earliest divertimento minuets. The trio, on the other hand, with its abrupt jerk from minor into major, is characteristic of his mature practice of planking down contrasting keys alongside each other, sometimes with sensitive poetry, here, as a kind of shock-tactic such as Beethoven loved to use. If the tune of the finale, with its syncopations and sharpened fourth, is not a folk dance, it merely proves that folk melody and its turns of phrase had become an integral part of Haydn's musical thought and expression.

The C major Quartet, no. 3, is called the 'Emperor' because its slow movement is a set of variations on the Emperor's Hymn ('*Gott erhalte Franz den Kaiser*'), the great tune which Haydn gave to his country as a national anthem. But there is a regal quality about the work as a whole: a poise and majesty in its themes and a depth and volume of sound in which the orchestral richness which Haydn was striving after in the Op. 71 quartets is fully achieved. How wonderfully this new range of sound is used in the service of the design as a whole is seen in the first movement, where the principal theme, hardly less pervasive than the falling fifths of the D minor Quartet, is treated now in the purest vocal counterpoint, now boldly outlined against a backdrop of semiquaver figuration, and again, transmuted into a swaying, lurching folk dance, over a massive double drone in viola and cello. In the variations on the Emperor's Hymn Haydn simply lets one instrument after another play the tune, unaltered, but garlanded with figuration that sensitively characterizes the instruments involved; the lyrical grace of the first violin, embroidering its arabesques around the melody on the second, contrasts with the grave dignity of the cello and the brooding, plangent quality of the viola, marvellously reflected in the chromatic inflections of its accompaniment, as if the imaginative grasp of its essence and personality that had begun to grow on Haydn in the Op. 71 quartets had suddenly become fully alive. The final variation is a re-harmonization of the tune for all four instruments, almost Bach-like in the poignancy and subtlety of its harmonies. The minuet shows Haydn's mastery of the long, irregular paragraph, and once more, in the A minor trio, his love of major-minor contrasts, touched with poetry as the melody lifts, with a Schubertian gesture, into A major. The last movement shows a certain kinship with that of the G major, no. 1, for it starts in the tonic minor, in which it moves for most of its length on a persistent current of quaver triplets. But here there is contrast between the triplet flow and the grave, poignant theme, which in fact generates the forward movement of the music; and even after the recapitulation the emergence into C major is held back till the very end, when it comes with a touching sense of wonder and release.

The opening of no. 4 in B flat might be taken as a *locus classicus* of Haydn's mature handling of both instruments and thematic material. The lovely curving ascent of the first violin from the softly held chord on the lower strings sounds almost improvisatory in its spontaneity; but it is balanced by its answering sentence, and the whole paragraph grows outwards from the rhythm and melodic line of the melody with wonderful flexibility and continuity of phrase-structure and translucency of scoring, the viola once again raising its distinctive voice. And in place of a second subject there is a mirror image of the first, with the cello curving downwards against a held chord in violins and viola. If anything could be more beautiful than this, it is the free expansions and variations of both versions in the recapitulation. The *adagio* is a rapt meditation on its five-note opening theme, welling up from the deepest springs of Haydn's being. Towards the end it breaks off short, and the five-note theme returns in overlapping entries between the instruments, bringing a sudden tightening and intensification of utterance; here the technical device becomes one with emotional expression. The minuet is driven along by the rhythmic thrust of its initial phrase; the peasant-dance atmosphere of the trio is rarefied, in its second part, by subtle nuances of scoring. The main tune of the finale has the vernal freshness of an English song, and its part-writing is correspondingly vocal; possibly some evening with a London glee club may have stirred in Haydn's memory. But the design of the movement is something new: an apparently straight-forward A-B-A, major-minor-major pattern which, however, instead of ending after the repetition of the first section, suddenly gathers speed and takes off in an extended free development, gathering up elements from both parts of the movement in its flight.

The same thing, or something very like it, happens in the first movement of the D major, no. 5. It begins as a relaxed and lyrical *allegretto*, moving into its tonic minor, with the tune (or rather, a derivative of it) in the cello beneath a running counter-point in the first violin; then it returns to the major, pauses, and suddenly dances away in an *allegro* which catches up the minor middle section and sweeps it into the major, carrying it, and the entire movement with it, on to a new plane of vitality. For his slow movement Haydn chooses the bright, distant key of F sharp major, and here the *largo cantabile e mesto* unfolds its great shining curves, then (as the music reaches the dominant) folds them back again upon each other as theme and counter-theme before coming to rest in the new key.

Ex. 16 Largo

But this is only the starting point for a far more searching exploration into distant heights and depths of harmony before the music circles homeward again, viola and cello following each other through the darkness in a passage which shows that the ageing man who once declared that he had 'only just learned to write for wind instruments' now at last understood the viola too with all his mind and imagination. The warm-heartedness of the minuet is enlivened by the cross-accents of its second section and thrown into relief by the scudding greyness of the trio, in the tonic minor, once more a throw-back to his earliest days re-lived with a lifetime's experience behind him. In the final rustic dance, there is a prefatory flourish of chords, the village band strikes up in open fifths leading into a reiterated scrap of tune, and the music is off to one of the most tightly yet freely patterned sonata-form movements Haydn wrote in all his life.

The first movement of the E flat Quartet, no. 6, is even more original than that of his predecessor. It is a theme and variations. The theme is uttered in laconic phrases until the lilting expanded cadence of its final bars; the variations draw spare contrapuntal lines around its unadorned restatements, first by the second violin, then by the cello, then in imitation between first violin and lower strings; the last variation, again quickening to *allegro*, opens out into a full-scale fugue before calmly turning into a normal variation again. There is a touch of mystery, of hidden power and meaning, about the whole movement. The second movement is called a 'fantasia' and is again a profoundly original conception. Written without key signature for half its length, its gentle, meditative theme starts in what is in fact B major, but ranges through a succession of keys until its wanderings finally carry it home to the key in which it started; here – at last with a key signature – it settles and unfolds in flowing contrapuntal lines of the utmost serenity and beauty. With the minuet Haydn once again steps to the brink of the one-in-a-bar scherzo and beyond, carried along, in the wonderful *alternativo* (as the trio is called) by the current of its ascending and descending scales of E flat and their running counter-themes and harmonizations. The monothematic finale makes brilliant play with imitative overlappings of the five-note figure from which the entire movement springs.

There remain the two great quartets of Op. 77, all that Haydn had the strength to complete of the set commissioned by Prince Lobkowitz. In the first, in G, he can be regarded as continuing the line of 'first violin' quartets from where he left off in Op. 64, so much does he give to the instrument, and ask of it: in the dancing, singing measure of the first movement, the musing semiquaver figuration of the *adagio*, the leaping acrobatics of the scherzo-minuet and Hungarian finale. Yet nowhere in the great procession of his quartets is the quartet-writing, as such, more balanced, varied and rich in scoring. One could quote examples endlessly, from the demure set-to-partners between cello and first violin as the main theme of the first movement returns as second subject (a passage that recurs, charged with new tension and urgency, in the development), to the quicksilver dialogue between upper and lower strings near the end of the finale, throwing fresh light on the rhythm of the ubiquitous folk-dance tune that has sparked off the entire movement. This fusion of instruments lends its driving force to the thrust and spring of the scherzo (one cannot call it anything else), slewing abruptly round on its closing cadence into the E flat of the trio. But it is supremely manifested in the *adagio*, also in E flat, but moving in its solemn course to the confines of the known world of harmony, the spaciousness of its majestic phrases and its whole design intensified by the scoring, high and ethereal or fathomlessly dark, and once more using the viola with the most sensitive understanding.

The F major, no. 2, seems to gather together in itself all the other strands in the string quartet's evolution, in particular that pure, linear string-quartet writing in which each instrument brings its strand of melody, clear and distinct, to the texture of the whole. In this first movement this clarity of texture not only throws fresh lights and shadows on the principal theme, classic in its serenity and poise, as it moves into the dominant as second subject, but is also the essence of the development, especially as it moves questingly through a widening arc of keys on a little figure, inconspicuous on its first appearance, but which reveals itself as Haydn's personal 'fingerprint' (cf. Exs. 1(x) and 2):

Ex. 17

The second movement, labelled 'minuet' but an undisguised scherzo as in the G major, contrasts the brilliant rhythmic and instrumental fooling of its first section with the grave tenderness of its trio, for which Haydn has once again pivoted round on his tonic into the dark and remote flat-sixth, this time D flat. The *andante* is in D major, and so far as its key-scheme goes it is a rondo, with a first episode in A, the dominant, and a second in the tonic minor. But in fact it is an indivisible and unflawed unity, for the grave, quiet march which is its theme pervades it throughout from its opening statement – the final distillation of Haydn's two-part counterpoint – to the moment when the unfaltering tread falls silent and the music slowly floats clear of earth, for a visionary moment, in what is in fact a great written-out cadenza, before returning with quiet inevitability to the last, simply harmonized restatement of the theme. The last movement combines all the dash and fire of his Slavonic-dance finales with a close, monothematic sonata-form design and a wonderful intricacy of overlapping themes and rhythms: once more, a sublimation and fulfilment of all that had gone before.

It was indeed the last, for he had no longer, at seventy, the stamina for such sustained musical concentration as a movement such as this requires. The two middle movements of the third, unfinished quartet were eventually published as Op. 103. As the key of the minuet indicates, the work would have been in D minor; the slow movement, a gentle *andante*, is in B flat major, with a middle section beginning in G flat – another sharp contrast of keys – and circling through a wide arc of modulations before returning home. The reiterations of the opening phrase with which the movement ends are charged with valedictory sadness, but its mastery of design and part-writing show no trace of failing strength. Still less does the D minor minuet – a true minuet this time, not a scherzo – a strange and potent cry of passion and pain, with its restless harmonies, tensely overlapping phrases, and the fiery uprush of its final bars; the last incandescence of the flame now held captive within the failing body.

Haydn wrote his string quartets in a world in which public concerts were a comparative rarity and chamber music was in the first instance enjoyed by playing it at home. And, though we know that some of them at least were written with his professional friends in mind, they remain within the capacities of amateurs. From then until now they have been the daily bread of the amateur quartet team, and it is by such amateur teams that they have been most truly known and loved. But now the radio brings this essentially intimate music back from the recital room into the homes of the many music-lovers who are not performing musicians. For them, it presents a twofold opportunity. It enables them to watch the processes of musical thought at their most transparent (and incidentally, there is no better way of teaching oneself to follow and to read a score). At the same time it brings them into close contact with a mind and personality of the utmost integrity, originality and native warmth. Eric Blom wrote of Mozart that 'there is no composer with whom familiarity breeds greater love and respect'. No one can live with these quartets without wanting to apply the same words to Haydn.